the grass in our childhoods

m. r. s. reverie

BookLeaf Publishing

Presentation by *BookLeaf Publishing*

Web: www.bookleafpub.com

E-mail: info@bookleafpub.com

ISBN: 9789357748711

First edition 2023

for Kayra, Karissa, Gabe

and all that our backyard taught us

PREFACE

It was best said by Wordsworth:

"Come forth into the light of things,
Let Nature be your teacher."

Replanted

It was at the nadir of my downward spiral when
I saw it: how much I hated myself
The meretricious way my subconscious talked
like a covert narcissist
The compunction I lacked for every insensible
choice I committed

So I set flame to the ignorant yellow dress
I addressed letters to the wind, letting it take
them where they needed to go

I traded self-pity for self-awareness
self-awareness bred despair
despair gave way to healing
healing made for battle scars
and a newborn mind
climbed through the fault lines of melancholy

A revolutionized baby eager to fill its head with
instruction from Mother Earth,
I looked to the sky and prayed it teach me life
through enlightened eyes

Replanted like the daisies between sidewalk
cracks,
I too have grown quietly through the gray

Ode to 'Autumn Leaves'

and there I was at the bottom
of rock and evolutionary block
late October autumn
leaves left bare trees

whole when empty
complete by season, crime-less treason
apple of my envy
worth found in rebirth

plotting to kill death,
or am I over? under headstone and clover
agony laced last breath
a baby bird's melody my final daytime reverie

too soon he took his bow
and by the grace of its wing I willed it to sing
it can't be over now
if baby bird in the tree devotes encores to me

Summer came in on an orange flame

Summer came in on an orange flame
her hot breath caressed my cheek
a kiss from under the greylag's wing
thus far my soul a stranger to my body

the same fingers that paint tulips pink
make a marionette out of me;
the string appeals to my anatomy
moving, breathing, being all by summer's hand

white is the world in her absence
but, still, she meets me under the sea
where we summon the birth of Aphrodite
looking at her face is looking in the mirror

I find myself in summer's daises sprouted
yellow
all that she sows I'm blessed to reap it
yet hapless to have to keep myself a secret
let every summer speak to my sincerity

When I feel lost I wander to the coast

When I feel lost I wander to the coast
where as empty as I am, I'm whole the most

I search for myself and for harmony
the salt water and air my armory

and peace whispers in cadence divine,
"find me always where the ocean kisses the
sky."

The way I see it

The way I see it, the ocean, in her enigmatic
beauty and unfathomable power,
is miserable.

And why shouldn't she be?
With all the energy she spends surrounding
Earth in a historic hug,
The house she is for countless creatures,
the home she is for wandering souls

A most gracious host, the ocean gifts
munificently to all who visit her shores.
She invites us into her space for comfort at our
worst
and offers ears to our ranting, raging, laughing,
crying, rejoicing—
She was there for your bad day, your breakup,
and grievances— for your friendly bonfires and
every beach wedding

The ocean empathizes and gives relentlessly,
especially since the habit is forced on her.
The moon, chief puppeteer of water's
undulation, has cursed the ocean with a
proclivity to feel everything, to fix everything

We use her as the crypt for our skeletons and
repay her with pollution, we tread her at surface
level though she holds boundless depth

The ocean is miserable.
She screams, throws tantrums, revokes her
precious gifts. She raises waves and brings down
ships.
Though impossible to find her teardrops, her
sobs are bleating reflections of a brutally
borrowed soul that nobody can refill.
Yes, there's countless portraits, infinite odes, and
endless admiration. It isn't enough, though.

The ocean holds us in a manner that connects
our aging bodies to the womb—
but who could hold the ocean?
listen to the listener?
empathize with the empath?
who holds the ocean?
Every hand in tandem is insufficient.

Near and far from the coastline, I see myself in
her shades of blue;
I am the ocean, you are the moon.

The Contentment of a Rock

A rock is most sanguine being a rock

basking in the sun,
a seat for a bird to perch,
a bridge for a snake to cross,
magnets for life like sand-covered tongues.

without air, my lungs obsolete
without ground, no place for my feet

A rock is proud of its nature

fulfilled where it sits,
willing where the wind takes it,
comfortable skipping waters,
puzzle pieces of the living world.

I wish to feel my feet belong where they walk,
I wish for myself the contentment of a rock

and I find Time cruel

I watch the sunrise
and miss the moon

an eye-blink ago she was threaded together by
spools of stars, muffling my ears from the war

her glowing eye watched over me while Mother
cried,

and I find Time cruel for pulling off the blanket
and shutting the moon eye when I opened mine

the war is never over
the sun is the catalyst
He brings yesterday into today

where I sit front row and watch you go back and
forth in your tennis match,
playing a game where love means no one is
winning

24 hours a day you play
24 years of love
24-love
no one's winning

especially the brother and sisters you stay for,
who all want to leave, but refuse responsibility
for your unhappiness in our absence

I fear a war without your little referees calling
double faults and mediating

perhaps the very reason we're all peacemakers
and pacifists

and I find Time cruel for intertwining your lives
if the only purpose is mine

colors drain from your faces the same way they
do the sky,

and once again we fall victim to Time's hand as
he turns the dial back to night

where I tuck myself under the sky and wish back
my ignorance from when I was a blind child

when you used to fuel my fairytales, but now I
doubt I'll ever wear a ring

though he's relentless in what he takes, Time is
merciful in his warning

for now I understand that even the sky and moon
are only married until morning

intentions > actions > words

11

if actions speak louder than words,
intentions are bellowing screams
from tombstones of regret
from ethereal hearts
from nature herself
from God himself

Water, Feed, Repeat

We planted seeds in early Spring
and said grace over them;
maybe to consecrate our intentions,
or just to hope for a lasting harvest

Rosé down our throats, we danced for the rose
buds,
and we danced for new beginnings.
Something new to grow with; something new to
love.
We watered the space together and so I loved
you too

When Summer came,
our garden was in full bloom.
Autonomous from air, my lungs filled with
flora, fascination, and you

so simple it was to intertwine our routines:
water, feed, repeat
we recovered when carnations dried in the sun,
but they were only the first victims of
destruction

Autumn nights grew cold, but hearts grew colder

my mind went dumb with quotidian rituals,
and life became miserably mundane
water, feed, repeat

the garden vs. time and I couldn't help the
underdog
my religious knees bled, I bent until my back
broke,
my eyes were water pales in vain
water, feed, repeat, water, feed, repeat, repeat,
repeat

Winter took the remaining life to her mouth
frost bitten flowers kept fruitlessly
yet like a waterfall,
my heart gave with futile drudgery

Every ounce of care, but it took more effort to
quit,
so I gave you every reason to give up
while I stirred with my feelings
as lasting as the seasons that dictate them

Little Bird

Little Bird perches in a tree and sings her little
song;
she keeps to herself 'cause that's where she
belongs

On the wings of autonomy, she flies and perches
alone
as far as she's aware, no greater love is known

See, Little Bird, knows a thing or two about
feelings like the weather
for the pulchritude of her feathers

The hunters wrapped around her finger, and
Little Bird wrapped around their minds,
right in the sweet spot, she's learned not to cross
that line

Victim to emotional fatality,
her facade is just so much more captivating than
her personality

I feel for Little Bird; I see her and see me:
a mere dream, a fantasy, and I let myself be

Only meant for show,
never to get to know;

that's when the obsession stops.
When the fluttering flower you've been
fantasizing actually talks

about my night dreams and what they mean
and where my daydreams can lead;

never understanding how my brain is two
enemies,
or why it's a soundtrack from the 1970s.

But, a yearner for romance, I'll toss my hair and
flirt;
you'll pursue me and I'll get hurt

Somehow my naivety leads me to surprise,
though it happens every time.

I'm the left you make on your way to Mrs.
Right,
I'm the sunset you chase just to reach the sky at
night

Your fascination for me fades as time goes on,
but I promise I can be interesting with my
clothes on

Like Little Bird, I have so many songs left to
sing,
but can't get anyone to keep listening

Was it out of tune? Should I try a different key?
Give me a chance to change the melody

How do I make my words music to your ears?
How do I train my voice to be something you
want to hear?

Please, Little Bird and I never know what we're
doing wrong
Maybe if we'd hidden in the trees, but all we did
was sing our song

Sun, Sadness, and Me

I sat atop a greening hill
to romanticize my tear spills
and Sun spoke to me:

"Who did this to you, child?"

"It was Sadness, Sun. Sadness took watercolors
to my face—
her brushstrokes of anguish and grace—
isn't it magnificent? Such deep blues!"

"I prefer happier hues."

"But what complexity is behind yellow and
orange and even gold?
Sadness' blues run deep from warm to cold.
No offense, Sun, for you're beautiful, but
stagnant and simple too.
What is there to learn from you?"

"Just that. Simplicity. The will to be happy. Why
don't you look up at me?"

"I go blind looking at the bright side."

"Then close your eyes; see me with your skin
and your ears.
What do you feel? What do you hear?"

With a reluctant sigh,
I closed my eyes,
and braved the blazing sky.

"At this third hour, I hear folk strings
harmonize when the cardinal sings,
and the breeze of a tree swaying to the song.
I feel the grass heat under my bare feet, and
aspiration carried for miles long.

I'm safe in your space of sunlit sappiness,
but what is there to gain in the state of
happiness?
I am inert here; I don't change. I don't grow."

"The very lesson of my yellow
is to take life slow—
feel my warmth to your bone.
See the shadow I give you so
you don't dance alone.

Let some days be simple, let yourself be still.
Romanticize your blue, but see my gold as
Petrarch's quill.

You need both, dear child, Sadness and me,
too—
like the Earth needs me when the sky is blue.
Look how your tears glisten in my light, how
much to the painting I add!"

"Perhaps the art is isn't right without both happy
and sad. Without the two, the portrait is
incomplete."

"Without the three."

"Ah, yes; the three: Sun, Sadness, and Me."

Enraptured in a new romance, before the earth
faded back to umber, I ran with the air in the
tree.
The wind asked my hair to dance, and they did a
sort of swinging number, and I felt free.

Itinerant Dreamer

20

Itinerant dreamer
with no itinerary
but to follow the sun

Underground, the Invisible Tree

I.
underground, the invisible tree
roots itself in perfect symmetry
a reflection buried in secrecy

twins of a whole
one, a body, the other, a soul
and the soul coaxes the body out of control

roots, in need of wisdom, further their frame
so the mirror-image is true, the tree does the
same
the two growing divergently with opposite aims

the tree on earth operates by subconscious
and tree roots seem to almost be osseous—
buried underground with the will of the
conscious

for people, flustered minds make for a turbulent
squall
i wonder if braided brains are what the stems
recall

and if the roots will remain when the tree takes
its fall

II.
underground, the invisible mind
weaves its veins into a bind
overlapping thoughts until they're hard to find

two halves of the same brain,
the underground reflection slightly less sane,
yet both subject to the same pain.

one body thinking in two ways it's always
known
the deeper i've thought, the higher i've grown,
but the mind of my body gained a mind of its
own

an instinctive one that talks without the need to
think
and upon interaction wills the aware mind to
shrink,
leaving the faces in the mirror terribly out of
sync

in nature's show, tangled roots make for crooked
trees
i wonder if my mind's song is the sapling's
reprise

and if thoughts will linger when my body finds
eternal peace

III.
nature's duality found in every manifestation
the tree and the brain a symbiotic combination
life to dust— an ode to creation

both minds to unlearn in new life forms
both bodies left to feed the worms

Insults from the subconscious

24

You had me by your teeth; I thought I misheard,
but you meant it as insult: "you love your
words."
I simply flew away from your pride in the
absurd
For the feline is my favorite, but I rule in favor
of the bird.

A True Story (told in the style of a long question)

What does it mean when a bird gives you its
feather?

When you've been drowning in a glass half
empty, so you take a walk and not the
bottomless sky or even the infinite wildflowers
lighting your path can fill you up again,
so your eyes are pooling,
but refusing to spill,
refusing to permeate the glass with any more
hopelessness,
refusing to give sadness another win,
but inching closer to despondence with
every footstep,

and you come to a crossroads at the streets of
Dejection and Persistence, and
both paths are long and windy with rollercoaster
hills so you might as well choose Dejection if
it's what you feel anyway,

and as you embark on its treachery, a bird,
graceful and free,

flies so close to your face it could land on your
nose, but instead it treads the air in front of your
eyes,
and flaps its wing forcing a feather to fall in
such slow motion you think you're dreaming,
but you stick your hand out because somehow it
feels like a gift and it lands perfectly in your
palm
and your awestruck fingers wrap around it
to wrap your head around it
and your pooling wide eyes finally spill,
but not with sadness,
with reverence for a gift—
once a feather, now a gift;

and so the path of Dejection becomes the path of
Hope,
and you brave treachery with lighter feet,
and you wonder if the bird would've met you
with his gift on the path of Persistence or if hope
only comes at your lowest point,
and your mind tries to identify the bird,
and your phone tries to load results for "feather
symbolism,"
and you're desperate to know what it all means,
but why does it have to mean anything
but gratitude for the bird who saw you
drowning in your sadness
and gave you its feather to tread
a little lighter?

Ant Armies

Not too long ago I sat with my feet in the dirt, as
I do,
and marveled at a sight I've never seen:
two ant armies in parallel lines defending their
homes

Not one ant of either side stepped out of place,
not one threatened to attack,
though they stood militantly and remained
vigilant

Perhaps humans have made things too
complicated, and defense can be found in
pacifism

the grass in our childhoods

I get up early, I kiss mother's cheek, and ready
myself to learn
inevitably different than the way you do, though
it shouldn't be

The classroom is my backyard and the beach
and the mountaintops I haven't seen
My teachers are the sky and the ocean and the
trees I can't yet reach

In the palm of nature's hand I sit.
I listen to whispers from the wind, and watch the
necessity of change lest we live in extremes,
and I pray alacrity to my feet in times of
stagnancy

On nature's shoulders I stand.
I witness the moon in all her phases, discerning
that the only consistency we can be sure of is
change,
and I pray peace to my soul in constant
uncertainty.

In the pit of nature's belly I stir
with the storm coming for my burning brain

loving that the sun does not last forever,
and I pray liberation to a mind combusting blue.

and I pray gratitude to the grass in our
childhoods
that first taught us to be barefoot and free,
to stretch our arms and cut through the air
staining our memories with childlike ease

and still I touch the grass and relate to the grass
and am the grass
and I hum with my ear
                to the earth,
Her heartbeat keeping time

The Next Time You Feel Insignificant

The next time you feel insignificant against the
night sky,
connect the stars and see the blueprint for bodies
is drawn from nature

connect emotions to the moon
who includes us in magnetic fields
connect existence to intention
and find purpose in feeling small

how unfathomable it is that every being
past, present, and future
is a piece to the universe's cosmic puzzle
how vital we are
to keep continuation whole

when I stand under infinity, in all of its awesome
capabilities, I do feel small,
but I don't feel unimportant

I feel part of something;
included in a journey not entirely mine.
I can't think of a more profound way to live

So when the eye made from stars and galaxies
looks out for me, I look back with belonging

and the moon is waning,
and I am waiting
to take my place in the night sky